Logo Design

How to Create a Catchy Logo

by Josh Cooper

Table of Contents

Introduction

Logo designing is very important part of graphic designing. The logo is the visual entity that signifies an organization. A logo must be functionally extended to every kind of intercommunication as the central material of a complex identification system of an organization. The design and incorporation of logos in a visual identity system, therefore, is one of the most difficult and important fields of graphic design. Logos fall into three classifications that can be combined as well. Ideographs are completely abstract forms where pictographs are representational and iconic designs and logotypes, commonly known as wordmarks depict the company initials. It is counterproductive to redesign logos frequently because logos are meant to represent corporate identities of different companies fostering their immediate customer recognition. In that case, how can we ever accomplish the creation of an effective logo?

You can create a powerful toolbox taking help from the logo design showcases, resources, and tutorials posted across the Web for your creative logo designs. Firstly, you need to gain a solid understanding of the qualities of a good logo design. Secondly, stuffs you need to consider before initializing using the toolbox. In this guide, we will have you get down to the basics of what makes an effective logo design. Also, we will guide you through the principles of how to create an iconic brand identity.

Chapter one: What Is a Logo?

We must understand is the primary purpose of logos firstly to understand what a logo is. The aim of the design process is to make the logo immediately recognizable. It should inspire trust, loyalty, and superiority. The logo is one aspect of the commercial brand of any company or even economic entity. The various shapes, fancy fonts, colors, and images are strikingly different from other logos usually in the same market niche. Basically, logos are utilized to identify the brands and rarely describe a business. A logo generally, derives meaning from the quality of the product it symbolizes. A logo might be important than the signified product but what it represents is more crucial than its looks. The subject matter includes almost everything for logos.

What Makes A Good Logo?

A good logo is practical, appropriate, and simple in form conveying the intended message of the owner. Usually, it is the concept behind an effective logo that communicates the intended message. The design of a logo should effective enough to be printed at any size and even without color. A great concept and its execution are essential for a great logo.

Logo Design Process

Seeing only the result of the efforts of a designer can make it look like the logo creation is quite a simple task. Nevertheless, logo takes abrupt thought and creativity with combined elements to make an effective one. Follow a process when creating a logo ensuring the final design that meets the needs of the clients. We have enlisted some typical processes below that are mostly followed by professional logo designers. You will eventually develop your own with more practice.

o   Design brief

Conduct an interview for the design brief from the client.

o   Research

Conduct research on the industry also, its history and its competitors. Problem-solving issues should be considered first and later the design. Also, convey a research on successful logo design on current styles and trends related to the design brief. Follow trends to be aware of them as longevity in logo design is the key.

o   Conceptualize and Sketching

The single most important part includes developing the logo design concepts of the design process. Get creative around the design brief and performed research. You should start with sketching that is not time-consuming and a really good way to put ideas right on paper. And it is always easier after that to actually design it on the computer. You will always start from white paper once your imagination evolves through sketching.

o   Reflection

Taking breaks throughout the designing process helps your ideas to mature. It also renews the enthusiasm allowing you to solicit feedback. It also provides a fresh perspective on your logo creating work.

o   Revisions and positioning

Revise and improvise the logo only as required whether you position yourself by getting instructions from the client as a contractor or build a long-term relationship by guiding the client to the best solution.

o   Presentation

You should present your best logo designs to your client only. Usually, PDF format tends to work best but you may also wish to show the logo in context. This will help the client visualize the brand identity more clearly. You need to prepare a high-quality presentation to get your clients in the single most effective way to approve your designs. The meaningful presentation for a particular person is custom designed and not canned for a particular purpose. For a designer presenting a new idea is one of the most difficult tasks perhaps. However, everything done by a designer involves a presentation on how the design may explain itself in the suitable marketplace.

o   Delivery and support

You need to deliver the appropriate files and necessary support to your clients.

Chapter Two: Principles of Effective Logo Design Link: Things to Consider When Designing a Logo

Effective Logo Design

A good logo is simple, singular and appropriate in form conveying the intended message of the owner. You should pursue these five principles for ensuring that your design meets all of these mentioned criteria:

1.   When Designing a Logo Make Sure it is Simple

Good logos are unexpected and unique. It is barely overdrawn and easily recognizable. Simplicity makes a logo design versatile and quite memorable. The principle of design features keeping it simple that conveys an important design consideration. Simple logos are often easily recognized, memorable and effective in conveying the requirements of the client. A precise and distilled identity used for promotion, advertising, and marketing will easily catch the attention of a viewer. For example, Nike the largest shoe manufacturer in the world, the basis of effective international branding for it is quite a simple graphic.

The point of keeping it simple is that a logo is not a testing ground for your typography and illustration skills. It is rather a test of your presentation sense and design insight. The logo most of the time does not require a caption or even the name of the brand. But we know it the moment we take a look at it. You can use it on pamphlets and sign boards. We will not be confused about the identity of the brand if we do not use the brand name altogether. A complicated logo is difficult to identify resulting in failure in audience engaging. A logo is supposed to be an emblem that you need to keep simple.

2.   Make Your Logo Design Appeal to Different Audiences

An effective logo design achieved by keeping it simple should be memorable, yet appropriate. The subject matter of a logo surprisingly is of little importance relatively. Appropriate contents sometimes fail to play a significant role. But it does not mean that appropriateness is not desirable. It merely implies that a matched relationship between a symbol and the product it symbolized is objectionable under certain conditions and often impossible to achieve.

Flexibility and adaptability go a long way for designing or even art in helping you succeed. To put it in other words, one needs to be dynamic and not static. Rigidity in logo design only heads to zero scopes for improvement and innovation. With the death of innovation the design dies. As a result, the logo should be dynamic. But it does not mean it needs a change every week, rather a flexible approach. Companies expect their logo to claim to a differing spectrum of consumers. The audience with such diversity is bound to have different types of preferences and tastes. A rigid logo does not work in design.

3.   Timeless

An effective logo should be able to stand the test of time. Leave trends actively to the fashion industry to follow. Trends always come and end but longevity is the key when the brand identity is concerned. Stand out and make it timeless.

4.   Design a Unique Logo

By being uniquely identifiable a logo rises to prominence as an identity of a brand. To put things into perspective, consider apple-MacBook. Literal interpretations apart, a minor change was able to transform an otherwise boring Apple into one of the most iconic logo images. Instead of trying too hard to achieve uniqueness, you should aim to think something unique by bringing mundane objects into uniqueness.

5.   Make Sure Your Logo Design Is Versatile

An effective logo tends to work across a variety of applications and media. Logos should be structured in vector format for this reason ensuring any scale of size. It should be designed for all purposes including printed, reverse printed, the size of a stamp or even a billboard. One effective way for creating a versatile logo is to begin in black and white designs. Rather than color, this allows you to focus on the shape and concept being subjective in nature. Printing costs should be a major concern as the more colors are used the more expensive over the long term it will be for the business.

Working firstly in black and white ensures its look in its simplest form. As for colors very subjective, they can distract from the overall design. Setting a colorful logo might result in only responding toward the color of the design elements and not the composition. Reconsider submitting color suggestions for review to a client before they have signed off on a final design of a black and white logo. It is better to get familiarized with the commercial printing process. That way you can avoid encountering printing problems. Know the difference between the CMYK, RGB, and Pantone color systems.

Versatility works greatly in making a logo design popular. If your logo is such that it fits on posters but fails on coffee mugs, it will hardly achieve popularity. If your logo furthermore is a slave to a color scheme, it is not a good logo either. It means a logo should look fine even if it is displayed in black and white, or a set of colors that are not part of the actual design.

6.   A Logo Should Be Appropriate

Positioning the logo perfectly is appropriate for intended audience. For instance, the font and color scheme appropriate for a logo for a toy store are not really useful for a law firm. A logo lacks the need to express what a company does. Showing foods are not necessary for restaurant logos or showing teeth is not necessary for dentist logos. They might be relevant but you can do better. For example, the Mercedes logo or the Apple logo fit in these criteria.

A logo needs to be self-explanatory by the alliance with a product, a service, or a corporation only. Logo acquires its efficiency and meaning from the quality of symbolized matter. The logo will eventually be perceived as the second rate in case if a company is the second rate. Again, a logo will do its job barely before an audience immediately has been conditioned properly.

7.   Make Sure Your Logo Design Has a Story to Tell

Every logo has a story in the background. If you view a logo as an artwork or mere text, you will be unable to decipher the meaning behind the logo. A successful logo tells two stories ideally as in the obvious one, and of course, the hidden one. Generally, clients ask for a cool and outstanding logo. Basically, if you can depict the clients that the design of your logo consists of deep and meticulous ideology, they will love it regardless of it being simple. Let us take, for example, the logo of Toyota. The logo is nothing like three distinct ovals with a fancy 'T'. As per Toyota, each of the three ovals has its own hidden meaning. The center overlapping ovals represent the trust and faith between the company and its consumers. The outer encircling oval depicts the global expansion plans of Toyota. And the negative space complements the encircling oval while expressing the infinite reach of the overall logo and the company. When they are put together, it represents a steering wheel as symbolic of cars.

How Much Does A Logo Cost?

It is the one of the most frequently asked questions that cannot be easily answered. It varies over the needs of each company. The best approach for each client is to draw up a customized quote. When designing a logo take a number of factors into consideration, such as, the number of logo concepts needs to be presented with the number of revisions needed, and also the amount of research require compared to the size of the business and so on.

- Timeframe

Typically, logo design process should take four to fifteen days whereas some can go on for months. Think of a time length for your logo design to be used. Do you want it to be designed with much less research in less than a day? Your timeframe should vary according to that.

- Price

Usually, the cost of the utility reflects what you will receive. You get what you pay for most of the time but the price here is not the only indication.

- Affiliations

If you are affiliated with any design associations or publications then this is a good indication of a good dedication. It is not essential but it will help you in your craft.

Professionalism and communication

Present yourself with confidence. Get your professionalism at work. Try communicating more effectively like responding to your emails quick enough. Consider working with a contract that tends to protect both of you.

- Questions asked

Questions should revolve around your goals, target markets and history for a better success. Here are some essential questions you need to get familiar with when designing your first logo:

1. What types of logos are there?

Logos are separated into four categories:

- o Wordmarks are multi-letter abbreviation groupings or freestanding word comprising logotypes. Such as eBay, CNN, Google, and such.
- o Letterform logos are constituted of a single letter. For example, Uber, McDonald's and etc.
- o Pictorial logos are illustrated tokens of recognizable things. For instance, Starbucks, Playboy, and Twitter.
- o Abstract logos represent abstract art. Nike is the most famous brand to pull off an abstract logo successfully.

2. Which type of logo would best suit my company?

One type of logo barely works for everyone. The best fit depends a lot on the name and what you make. For example, for a short company like eBay wordmark logotype works pretty well. Generally, letterform and Wordmarks logos aid consumers remember the name better than abstract logos. However, opting for an abstract symbol must be straightforward and should mirror the personality of your brand.

3. The key points about my business that my logo should convey

From color to shape your logo should provide an immediate sense of the identity of your company. People should get a feel when they look at it for the distinctive point of view toward your brand personality. You need to express you are professional and different from your competitors. Make sure to point out a real business confidently and successfully. For instance, the logo of Amazon is represented by the name of the company itself. They have added an arrow below pointing from the 'a to z' that embodies brand identity of its namesake exceptionally well. The arrow also doubles as a smile conveying a friendly customer service while connecting the 'a to z'. It is because Amazon in actually offers everything A to Z.

4. What are the best logo colors?

The choice of color is extremely important. It is quite paramount to choose a color for best differentiating yourself that your biggest competitors avoid using in their logos. Different colors considerably pack different psychological punches. Such as, the color red is appropriately used in Red

Bull's logo. It is expressed as active, heightened and even a little more alarming. Yellow express happiness, freshness, and energy working as a wise choice for a company fixated on health and wellness. While blue used for Ford, and Samsung rather evokes confidence and reliability.

5. What fonts should I consider?

Like colors, fonts inspire and convey various emotions. Different types of fonts tend to work best for different businesses. A logo for a legal firm, for instance, conveying strength, and justice might be best represented in a straightforward font free of embellishment. On the other hand, a kid utility shop might opt rather for an eccentric font that expresses sweetness and fun communicating youth.

6. How much will it cost?

Typically, professional design firms for a logo alone charge somewhere between $4,000 and $15,000. This might not necessarily be in the budget for beginners or start-ups and rather small businesses. For a more affordable option contracting a freelance designer can be suggested. Look for someone depending on his or her level of experience charging between $35 and $150 per hour. But make sure you do not hire someone just because of their bargain price. Find a designer that is familiar with your required field and also your competition.

7. Where should I display my logo?

There are fair chances that you would want to show off your logo. So it is a better question where you should not display it. It can be pretty much everywhere. Try online by weaving your logo into your website, and on social-media sites. You can also display it on digital ad campaigns. Also offline will work with putting your logo on your front door, company stationary, business card, uniform and product packaging.

8. What are some mistakes to avoid?

Settling on a logo before seriously considering the logos of your key competitors is the worst mistake of all. If your logo ends up being similar even in the slightest to theirs, customers will fail to tell you apart and you could definitely lose business. You should also be cautious against sizing up your logo only on a piece of paper. That is opposed to envisioning it across several individual marketing spaces.

9. Is it too soon to worry about how my logo will look in 10 years?

Most logos need some touching up after a decade or so for avoiding growing stale. The key includes getting it right from the beginning and then fine tune as per need over time. Undergoing minor surgeries bunch of times from the core idea is still the same as the first design.

Chapter Three: Avoid These Mistakes When Designing a Logo

1. Do Not Underestimate Color in Your Logo Design

Colors form the essence of any kind of visual representation. Designers often overlook the importance of a cautious use of colors. Probably this is attributed due to the misconception of clean design where the only permissible color is white. But colors keep the power to affect both feelings and emotions. Your choice of color ideally should be chosen on the basis of the target demographic of consumers. Consider the age, gender and most importantly, cultural orientations of the target audience. Then use it to couple with your artistic creativity.

2. Do Not Over Innovate: Do Not Fall in the Cool Logo Creation Trap

This point works along with simplicity. Innovation is a blessing where you can experiment and work around to come up with the perfect idea for your logo. However, every kind of things has their own share of limits. Your innovation boundaries are limitless but their functional usage is often victimized by the possibilities of innovation provided by a given product. Excess experimentation can result in a gorgeous logo but might not be identifiable with the company itself. A logo is not at all an art masterpiece. Instead, your main aim is to make the logo identifiable while easily associated with the brand. Your design at the end of the day should be an identifier of a company the customers can easily identify. Your logo design is a success if you can accomplish the irrespective of it being generic. For example, take a look at Opera's logo consisting of just a red 'O'. People can easily identify that it belongs to Opera.

3. Do Not Underestimate Custom Typography in Your Logo Design

The typeface should be unique when it comes to logo design. A custom hand-drawn typeface is technically way better than most vivid fonts. Nothing can match a drop-dead beautiful font; you just have to spend time choosing the right one to use. It keeps the design plagiarists at bay if nothing else. That is because if not a custom typeface, your logo will be ripped within minutes once your font is discovered. For this reason, custom lettering must be the preferred way. Also, custom lettering is far more detectable in a logo than a purchased or downloaded font. Talking about fonts, Coca-Cola can be the best example.

4. Do Not Be Predictable: Create Smart Logo Designs

Make sure your logo is worth looking at while telling a story. On first look, your logo should convey the identity of the brand. Avoid making it too loud though, such that for an umbrella production firm your logo should not shout out "rain". Thereafter, your logo on a deeper look should also be suggestive of something. Again, consider the umbrella firm. It should refrain from mentioning rain or sunlight but suggestive of weather. Now if we put our attention to the Lion

Bird logo. It is the colorful bird with the brand name. The specialty is at the bird's feet where a lion's face is visible in the logo.

5. Top Logo Design Tip: Be Different

Recall the number of logos visible with either Helvetica or Papyrus employed. It pays to be unique when it comes to logo design. Just like any other variant of design, logo design has its own share of trends that keeps on falling in and out of favor over time. It makes sense in the case of steering clear of cliches giving the clients a unique expected logo from you.

Chapter Four: How to Design a Logo

Four Parts needs your attention in this process:

-       Brainstorming

-       Testing the Design

-       Finalizing the Design

-       Sample Logos

A great logo is way more than just images and words. It tells a story about your company; your identification, your work and what you stand for. That is considerably a lot to ask from one piece of art. For that reason, it is important for you to take the time for doing it right. But you are fortunate enough that you do not have to do it alone. The necessary steps below will help you through the entire designing process of a logo successfully branding you in the marketplace.

Part 1: Brainstorming

Step 1

Determine the primary function in the following process of your logo. A logo tends to represent your brand through the use of fonts, shape, color and images. You have to be specific about your need of a logo can guide your design.

-       Enhance admiration: If clients have a complete impression of your business already, by creating a logo you can build on that. It is well-regarded for its effective simplicity and good looks with cleverness.

•   Boost recognition: As a start off or a new company competing in a field with a lot of other players can be tough. Having a strong logo initially can help clients recognize your own brand more willingly.

•   Create trust: The most important part of bringing in clients and keeping them is based on their will for trusting you. A solid logo conveying your honesty and integrity is able to help put clients at ease.

•   Create memorability: Consumers shop mainly with their eyes and logos can be a great measure to remember rather than products, names, and services. A customer over the time comes to associate your logo with your company.

Step 2

Consider your target market. It is significant to be specific about your client and customize your logo to appeal to the user of your services. A logo for a law firm, for example, must communicate strength and integrity. But it should not necessarily look like that would work well for a simple catering company. A logo for a florist shop, in this case, could incorporate an eccentric font with a bright color scheme. This would absolutely not work so well for something like an auto body repair garage.

Step 3

Decide whether to incorporate the name of your company into the logo. Making the name part of your logo design to building name recognition for your business may not always be a good idea. Include the name in case it is reasonably distinctive but not when your goal is to create name recognition. Do not include the name in your logo if it is too long and generic or lacks personality. Also, if you are considering translation globally, this is a very bad idea. Again, if you must put your logo on a product like a sneaker or a handbag leave the name out. Think of all the different means you plan to use your logo. Picture the smallest possible size you may need. If the company name is fussy when the logo is the size of a thumbnail, it is best to put it out of the design.

Step 4

Follow the color pattern of your company. If your company has already settled the use of certain colors in its advertising and other materials, it is significant that those colors are reflected in the logo. Consistent use of colors establishes familiarity. You want consumers to be able to link your logo mentally to the company. Public develops a subconscious association with the specific colors your company has branded itself with. If you lack an established color scheme for your business, research on the psychology of colors for choosing appropriately. For example, red signifies passion, strength, energy and confidence but it also signifies danger.

Step 5

Be inspired by but skip copying successful logos. It might be alluring for creating something looking like your favorite corporate logo but it will obviously convey unintentionally that you are quite lazy and uninspired.

Look at logos of other similar businesses similar deciding what you like and dislike about them. Do not simply get overwhelmed while looking at examples. Ten or twelve should suffice to provide ideas of what to do and to avoid. A successful logo should be simple and timeless. Set these as goals as you continue playing around with ideas.

• When you are struggling for ideas, try using a different keyword for conducting searches online or use a thesaurus simply to point your thinking in some new directions.

• Doodling help sketching things out and playing around with them. Try writing keywords in different fonts to check if something visual sparks an idea.

Step 6

Designing a simple logo is an exercise in restraint. While you may try conveying a multitude of messages with your design, doing too much will result in sabotaging the success of your logo. Avoid using too many colors, layered images, and multiple fonts. A confusing or cluttered logo won't convey a clear message. The presence of too many visual elements in your logo will make it difficult for the customer to process. They will fail to know where to look or what it means.

A simple logo practically is easier and less expensive to reproduce. As your logo might appear on a variety of items starting from letterhead to advertisements to tote bags, a simplicity of it could save you money in the long run.

Part 2: Testing the Design

Step 1

Create multiple designs as you might want to express various ideas in your logo design. Commit them all to a paper which will allow you to see what works and what does not. Even a flop design can spark an idea offering one element for retaining in the next version of your logo design.

Step 2

Draw a rough sketch firstly of the design. It is better to put pencil to paper in the initial stages of the logo design process. Sketching is honestly a quick and easy way to put your ideas on the paper for evaluating them more easily. Plain white paper or graph paper can make good backgrounds for the trial of pencil sketches.

Designing is not a linear process so skip erasing. Keep the pages secured with the designs that you disliked. They may at any time spark an idea or offer something of value upon later examination. Large design companies tend to sketch out dozens of pages of logo concepts often before even touching a computer mouse. Take a tip from the pros for that matter and focus on your sketches.

Step 3

Show the design significantly to a test market. Moving forward once you have finally come up with a seemingly winning logo, but it is very important to get feedback first.

Step 4

Get feedback from your target market. Show your designs for your logo to a sampling of people fitting the profile of your ideal consumer. You may show them quite a multiple of designs or simply the strongest candidate. Ask key questions for revealing their reaction for your logo. Also, check which image or message of the logo tends to convey them. Again, whether they think it is easy to recognize and seems consistent with your company or your industry.

Step 5

Be alert of relying on family and friends too heavily. While you need an informal opinion of those close to you, their comments may not provide the kind of useful feedback. However, you can use the opinion of family and friends to test the memorability of your logo. Let them take a look at the design for a few seconds and then tell them to draw it. It is memorable if they can remember most of it.

Step 6

Make sure that the design has the possibility to scale. Consider all the different ways how you may use your logo. Let it be in newspaper ads or on signage and even on your website. Your logo has to function well whether reproduced in a large format or a small one. If a logo consists of too many thin details or lines then those elements might get lost. Or simply, the logo may look too fussy at rather small sizes.

If a logo is made to look good for only business card sizes then the possibility is it will appear clunky when reproduced in something larger. Graphic design programs, for instance,

Adobe Illustrator or Inkscape can allow you to examine the scalability of your design. Try making copies of your design if you are working by hand initially at different size settings.

Part 3: Finalizing the Design

Step 1

Creating a final draft covers your logo to be digitized. You can do this yourself either or hire a professional for you. The best solution is learning a graphic design program. Adobe Illustrator is the most used program but Inkscape is another offering that can be downloaded online for free. There are plenty of instructional books and also websites that can allow you to learn Illustrator. Community colleges besides some continuing education programs also offer graphics classes in this design program.

If you have a background in graphic arts already then computer-assisted design might work well for you to do alone. Also, you are in a case, a quick study then the possibility is that you may do it yourself. Otherwise, it is better off to put your work in the hands of a professional.

• Visit websites of designers to see their portfolios. You want to look for someone who has experience working with practical logo designs.

• You may go through revision with an artist or simply let them reproduce your idea. In any case, find out the necessary turnaround needed for your design until you see a finished product.

• Find out about possible costs. Again, where you are in your design processing steps will definitely impact the cost of the service. If you need them to go back to step one with you in your design, it must be more expensive. But of you are satisfied with the logo you created then simply have it professionally computerized.

• Check online services for a number of online graphic design services allowing you to pay a set fee and receive several logo designs in return from artists trying to win the job. You choose the best design for working with that artist through the completion of your project.

Step 2

Keep yourself open to listening. It is important once your logo is finished that you stay open to feedback on the design. Use of social media can abruptly help. If your company managed an established online presence then run the logo past connected people for listening to what they have to say.

• Try your logo out on the website first. For a negative response to your logo, easier and less expensive that you revise and republish it on your website rather than to redo already printed materials.

• Get remarkable details. If the logo is confusing or difficult to read to your clients then press them for details. The more you can get before you invest in all the print collaterals, the easier it will be to tease the design.

How to Design a Successful Business Logo

- Deciding On the Basics

- Drafting Your Logo

- Finalizing Your Logo

- A good logo design tends to go far in adding a positive feel to your business. You should make sure because of this that your logo is designed thoughtfully and leaves a positive impression to people wanting to do business with you. You need to be quite careful designing your logo. It is because the design is the identity of your company. The best thing will be making sure it is appealing and inspiring.

Part 1: Deciding On the Basics

Step 1

Focus on your message how you want to communicate to your audiences. Deciding on what you want people to think as they see your logo will inform the rest of your design process. Also, knowing about your potential and target audience for creating a design for them will bring your logo to a success. You have to make sure your logo design is quite relevant to your products and necessary services in the market. It will surely help you connect to your clients while building a positive image. Consider adding a remarkable tagline to your logo design conveying your message down to your target audiences.

Step 2

Decide on a logotype as they typically fall into three basic categories. They are usually font-based or abstract or simply illustrative. Font-based logos, for example, Coca-Cola logo use a unique type for differentiating themselves. In a literal way, illustrative logos show the works of the company, like a country club logo that depicts a golfer. While abstract logos, as in the Adidas logo, tend to serve only to visually attract the attention of the buyer but wholly linked to the brand through overall advertising. Abstract logos can be quite expensive. Their measure is to design while clearly associating them with your business. For a small business, however, the best choices are font-based logos and illustrative logos particularly.

Step 3

Considering the mood for your logo to convey is quite an important part of processing a logo. Different design choices within a logo are able to communicate different kind of feelings and a whole lot of qualities to a consumer. Certain qualities of your business can be reinforced in the mind of customers by making these design choices across a logo consistently. The shapes are capable of evoking different feelings for viewers for instance. Or circles tend to demonstrate unity and completeness. But squares only show stability and mere professionalism. Additionally, fonts styled as hand written can show creativity or humility but rather bold typeface fonts are capable of showing professionalism and elegance.

Step 4

Think about colors you want to use. Different colors just like shapes and fonts can reinforce the message of your logo. Each color tends to have its own particular set of moods.

Part 2: Drafting Your Logo

Step 1

Researching the logos of other successful businesses in your industry is a part of the process. Performing research on the logos of your healthy competitors will enable you to know about the trending logo designs and preferable styles in the industry. You can visually learn from the mistakes of your attended competitors and create an appreciable design. Consider the stuff that differentiates your brand more from that of your competitors trying to include it in the design. On the other hand, allow other logos to alter your design process. But getting an exclusive logo design will ensure the visual identity of your company. Your logo design must be such that your brand stands out from the competitors. So, giving the effort to avoid trends found in the logos of your competitors can result in successful design.

Step 2

Your logo needs to comprehend your business successfully from the competitors while being instantly memorizable. Ensure that your logo design is unique, meaningful, and memorable. Such a logo design is capable of grabbing the attention of customers instantly sticking in their minds for a long time.

Step 3

Before deciding on a design, learn that scaling is a big factor. Think of all those places and stuff where your logo will appear. This may start from brochures to advertisement billboards. A good logo should be exceptionally scalable while easy to reproduce. Ensure that it fits wherever you put it without it particularly being complicated and indecipherable when printed very small.

Step 4

Simplify your necessary color schemes. Many of the most successful logos only have used mostly one or two colors. Logos with more vibrant colors can appear visually confusing and overcomplicated. Some mediums additionally, only permits for two colors. So, try to design your logo limited to two or maximum three colors. But most importantly, do not forget to check your logo printed in black and white to see if it works.

Part 3: Finalizing Your Logo

Step 1

Understand that you need to hire a professional. Even if you are very confident, hiring a professional designer is basically the right move. A professional is able to give you a clean and reliable logo design suggesting any kind of improvements even in color. A designer, in addition, will know how well a design will transfer to print as well as the cost to print. These involve two crucial components only a professional designer is aware of. We understand that hiring a designer may seem expensive to you. But you can expense the cost over ten years. It is the estimated usable life of a logo. So ultimately, it will dramatically reduce the immediate cost.

Step 2

Perform online research to locate for hiring a professional logo design company. Concentrate on hiring an experienced logo design company for your business. Make sure that the company is teamed up with a number of professional designers. Concentrate on the online portfolios of the company for choosing one that has designed logos you are finding appealing. Have a vigorous idea of the mood and message to convey with your logo when you are scheduled to meet with the designers. Negotiate a contract specifying the number of revisions on the logo needs to be made, the number of interaction to have with the designer, and finally, the turnaround for the design process. Expect a cost of $2,000 to $12,000 or more for the professionally designed logo.

Step 3

Now that you have finished sweating off looking at the amount of money a professional design is going to cost you, it is time to hire a freelance designer. You can save your company plenty of money by simply opting for a freelance designer. These designers tend to charge between $35 and $150 per hour for their services. Be careful to look for one with a portfolio of impressive designs with a good reputation. As a suggestion, you can also hire a freelancer who designed logos for businesses in similar industries. Upwork, DesignCrowd, Freelancer.com can provide plenty of good freelancers.

Step 4

Once you have finalized your designed logo, trademark it. You need to make sure that no one else can have the access to use it. This logo, after all, represents your company. So, the smart step is to protect it by applying for a trademark with your own government. Be prepared to pay over $300 for the filing fee for a trademark.

How to Design a Band Logo

- Researching Ideas for Your Logo

- Sketching and Refining the Logo

- Presenting Your Band Logo

The logo of a band is a great way to brand. It allows customers to identify your work immediately. Also, it acts as tangible for consumers.

Method

Researching Ideas for Your Logo: Step 1

Consider similar logos of other bands for inspiration. Hopefully, this will provide you an idea of what you want. Avoid copying a logo while trying to pass it off as your design. You might find common themes that you could convert into a logo of your own.

Step 2

Commercially research for successfully designed logos knowing they will associate you in designing a logo for your band. Apply design traits from corporate logos to your design. But be careful for not borrowing too many traits from a corporate logo resulting in an infringing risk on a trademark.

Step 3

You will be surprised by the amount of feedback from your community you can receive from asking around. People in your music community have different kinds of opinions and knowledge of what works. Mention the name of the band while describing the sound of your band. Consider making a post on your Facebook page that can come out in a huge help. Ask for advice in the social media and thoughts for a band logo. The explanation for the sound of music can result in any images or ideas to come up. You can never guess what people might come up with. Or conveniently, you can even try to get some useful advice from local designers.

Step 4

Decide what kind of design elements will possibly fit your band. Some bands tend to simply use their band name in some captivating fonts as their logo. While other bands simply abbreviate their name using an image for their logo.

Step 5

Consider the current status of your band. A remarkable band logo can be used as a great marketing tool for bands yet to reach a larger audience. Design a logo that is appealing potentially to fan base and could help you reach them.

Method 2: Sketching and Refining the Logo Step 1

Begin brainstorming for drawing several designs with your pencil on paper. Imagining words and images is pretty good but the quickest results can occur once putting those ideas out on a paper. They key to designing, in the beginning, is to provide yourself with plenty of options in the first place. Stop worrying about the quality of the logo as much. You will hopefully be spending quality of time refining and expanding the designs you are satisfied with.

Step 2

Consult with your mates in the band for revising your favorite designs. They can help you to choose a handful of your hard-worked designs. Narrow down your selection to the maximum five or six logos. Cut each design out if it helps you laying them out next to one another. Now your step is to create variations of each and every design. Modify the original design, for example, by trying to make the logo simpler. In regards to graphics, color scheme, and different sizes try to balance each design.

Use simply one of the revisions for redrawing the original design rather into a cleaner logo. If the design for that matter has a mixture of both words and images then it is better to try stripping the design of one of these features.

Step 3

Show your ideas to your friends or band members. Spend an amount of time brainstorming with them about the designs. Take any feedback anybody has seriously had to offer. Have each member select their favorite piece out of the whole series of hard worked designs. Isolate each chosen design as a favorite piece from the band. After that, line up all the chosen designs. You can vote the pieces in and out for a further selection process. Some of your band members hopefully will discuss in details what they like or do not like about your logo designs. If they do not still bring it up then ask away.

Step 4

Continue with your revisions once narrowing your designs down to about three or four. You should still continue to modify and revise because you should not really alter the design too many times. At this stage, go for subtle changes. For instance, making a line thicker or skinnier or inverting into color and black and white. Share the newest revisions with your band members to gather their thoughts. Repeat the process if everyone is still in disagreement and make more drastic changes to the designs.

Method 3

Presenting Your Band Logo step 1

Gain access to use a scanner to scan your logo to a computer. It is not required but helps if you have access to photo editing software like Photoshop. If you do not have access to any scanner, an office supply store can help. You can scan your photo from these stores to your desired quality. Just store the design either on a Pendrive or simply in the cloud.

Step 2

There are quality photo editing software options. Most of them are not Photoshop but Photoshop is considered as the industry standard. But there are plenty of free alternative software. You can download GIMP or Pixlr and other software on your computer. But make sure you have checked out each specification of the programs for compatibility with your machine.

Step 3

You can make adjustments to the logo once the image is in your editing software. Play around with filters for making digital revisions. You can vary the colors or add the text of the name of your band. These easy tools can potentially add a lot to your logo. One of the good things is that you can remove any white space with this software. You will be able to add the logo of your band by deleting white space to any flyer regardless of the color. A useful image type is .tiff for your use. You can also modify the quality of the image.

Step 4

Publish the logo online by adding them to your web pages. Set the logo as the profile picture of the social media pages of the band. Add the logo confidently to any upcoming show flyers. Get the word out through the blessing of the internet.

Step 5

You can carefully begin to print the logo onto merchandise once you and your band are satisfied with the band logo quite completely. Use the logo anywhere you want to. Let it be in the t-shirts, your newest albums, stickers, pins and absolutely everywhere. The best place to place a band logo, however, is on the back of an album. Or you can put it on an album cover. The options are truly limitless once you have created a successful logo. The key is to stick around with the logo and the name of your band. It is because the logo will not be as effective if you happen to change anything.

Tips

o   Find a symbol for your band as an option, for instance, the hooked cross from Blue Oyster Cult.

o   Once you have decided on a font sticking to it is best.

o   Once you have decided your genre, making the band logo more fitting to the music style is the perfect step. For example, Ingested's logo for brutal death.

o   Make sure to avoid making it too similar to some logo of another band

Conclusion

It is a complete misconception that logo design is an easy process. A logo, to begin with, is not just a mixture of some fonts and fancy colors put together. It is an identity of a brand to such extent that a logo is more identifiable than the name of the actual brand. Great logos are easily recognizable but we barely easy to create. There are many things to consider from concept to color for breaking down to a single emblem. You have to work a bit hard to get a successful logo for your purpose of work. We have tried to have you go through a number of details in this process. The key is to keep the logo simple, hide the meaning behind the quite impressive composure of shapes and colors. Researching the logos of other successful companies is a part of the process. The more you perform research on the logos the more you will know about the trending logo designs and preferable styles. With some help and desirable opinions, you can visually learn from the mistakes. Consider the stuff differentiating your brand more from that of your competitors. Getting an exclusive logo design will ensure the visual identity of your company. Your logo design must be such that your brand stands out. Provide more effort and you will get a successful design.